All the World Praises You!

an illuminated Aleph-Bet book
כֹּל הָעוֹלָם יְהַלֵּל יָהּ!

by Debra Band

with new translations by
Arnold J. Band

Copyright © 2018 by Debra Band

Firs

No   duced or transmitted in any form or by any other means, electronic or mechanical,
incl   any information storage or retrieval system, except for brief passages in connection with
a cr   on in writing from the publisher:

Hor
dba
www

Typ   ns Caslon. Typeset Hebrew text set in Davka Drogolin.

Con   Band
Prin   h Four Colour Print Group, Louisville, Kentucky

12 13 14 15 16 17   10 9 8 7 6 5 4 3 2 1

ISBN 978-0-9857996-7-0

Library of Congress Control Number: 2017912903

 *T*his book belongs to

For Dalia

*The publication of this book
was made possible by a generous gift from
Sharon and Steven Lieberman*

*in honor of their children
Benjamin Shai, Jessica Michal,
Rachel Shoshana and Jaryn Horner*

Alef

'Erets ≈ אֶרֶץ ≈ Earth

'Erets 'omeret: La'Adonai
ha'arets umelo'ah
Tevel veyoshvey vah.

Earth says: The Earth is the Lord's and everything it holds, the world and all who live on it.

Bet

Barak ❧ בָּרָק ❧ Lightning

Habarak 'omer:

Ma'ale nesi'im miketsey ha'arets

Berakim lamatar 'asa

Motsey ru'ah me'otsrotav.

The lightning says:
He makes the storm clouds soar
from the ends of the Earth;
He makes lightning for the rainstorm;
He releases the winds from His vaults.

גֶּשֶׁם אוֹמֵר: גֶּשֶׁם נְדָבוֹת תָּנִיף אֱלֹהִים

נַחֲלָתְךָ וְנִלְאָה אַתָּה כוֹנַנְתָּהּ:

The rain says: You have showered us with abundant rain, O God; when Your land was exhausted You brought it back to life.

Gimel

Geshem ✡ גֶּשֶׁם ✡ Rain

Geshem 'omer:

Geshem nedavot tanif 'elohim,

Nahalatkha venil'a 'ata khonantah.

ד

Daled

Desheh ❧ דֶּשֶׁא ❧ Grass

Yehi khevod ’Adonai le‘olam

Yismaḥ ’Adonai bema‘asav.

Deshaim ’omrim:

Yehi khevod ’Adonai le‘olam

Yismaḥ ’Adonai bema‘asav.

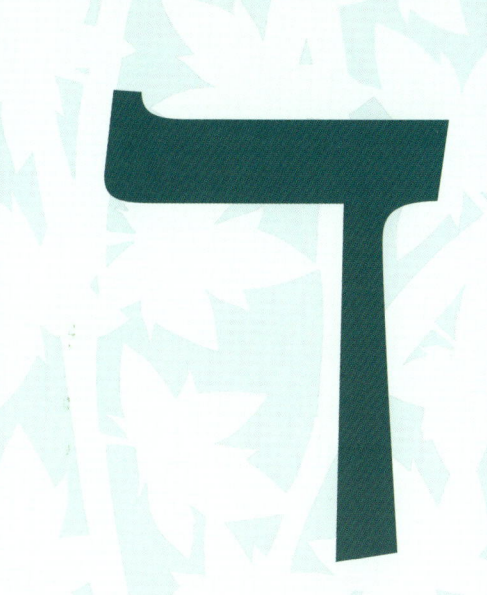

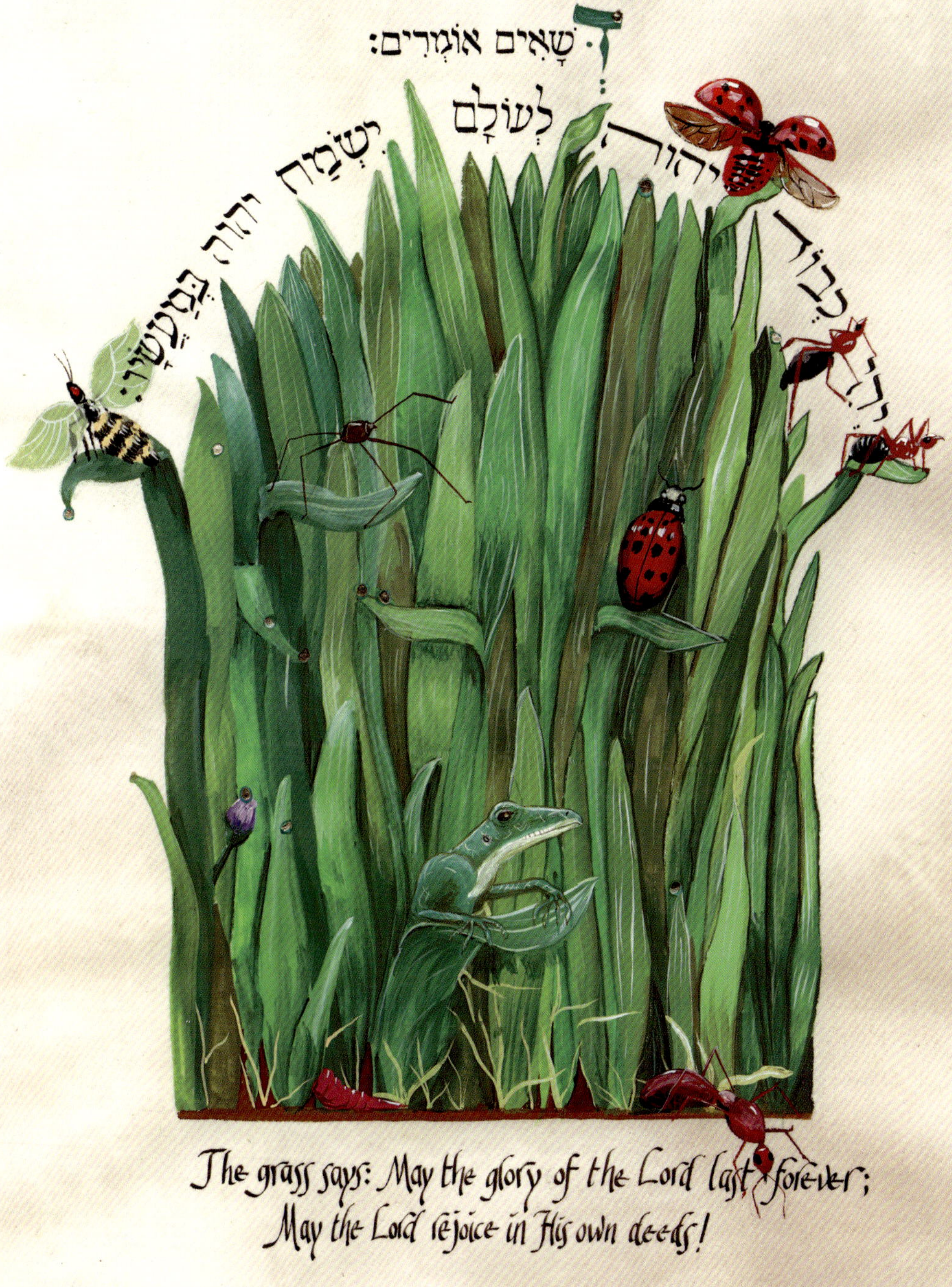
דשאים אומרים:
יהי כבוד יהוה לעולם ישמח יהוה במעשיו:
The grass says: May the glory of the Lord last forever;
May the Lord rejoice in His own deeds!

He

Hod ✡ הוֹד ✡ Splendor

Hod 'omer:

Hadar kevod hodekha

Vedivre nifle'otekha 'asiḥa

Vav

Vered ≈ וֶרֶד ≈ Rose

Havered 'omer:
Vayomer 'elohim tadshey ha'arets deshe
'Esev mazri'a zera
Etz pri 'oseh pri 'al ha'arets—
vayehi khen

הַוֶרֶד אוֹמֵר:
וַיֹּאמֶר אֱלֹהִים
תַּדְשֵׁא הָאָרֶץ דֶּשֶׁא
עֵשֶׂב מַזְרִיעַ זֶרַע
עֵץ פְּרִי עֹשֶׂה פְּרִי לְמִינוֹ
אֲשֶׁר זַרְעוֹ-בוֹ עַל-הָאָרֶץ
וַיְהִי-כֵן:

The rose says:
God said: Let the earth sprout vegetation,
Seed-bearing plants,
And fruit trees
of every kind on the earth.
And it was so.

הַזַּיִת אוֹמֵר אֶשְׁתְּךָ כְּגֶפֶן פֹּרִיָּה בְּיַרְכְּתֵי בֵיתֶךָ בָּנֶיךָ כִּשְׁתִלֵי זֵיתִים סָבִיב לְשֻׁלְחָנֶךָ׃

The Olive Tree says:
May your wife be like a fruitful vine over your home;
your children, like olive shoots around your table.

Zayin

Zayit ❧ זַיִת ❧ Olive

Hazayit 'omer:
Eshtekha kegefen poriya
beyarketey vetekha
Banekha kishtiley zetim saviv
leshulḥanekha.

Ḥet

Ḥipushit אִ חִיפּוּשִׁית אִ Beetle

Haḥipushit 'omeret:
Ma rabu ma'sekha Adonai
Kulam beḥokhma 'asita
Mele'a ha'aretz kinyanekha.

הַחִפּוּשִׁית אוֹמֶרֶת:
מָה-רַבּוּ מַעֲשֶׂיךָ יהוה
כֻּלָּם בְּחָכְמָה עָשִׂיתָ
מָלְאָה הָאָרֶץ קִנְיָנֶךָ:

The Beetle says:
How many are your deeds, O Lord
You did them all with wisdom.
The earth swarms with Your creatures.

טַל אוֹמֵר:
אֶהְיֶה כַטַּל
לְיִשְׂרָאֵל
יִפְרַח כַּשּׁוֹשַׁנָּה
וְיַךְ שָׁרָשָׁיו כַּלְּבָנוֹן:

The Dew says:
I shall be like the gentle dew
to Israel:
It shall blossom like a lily,
And strike root like a cedar.

ט

Tet

Tal טַל Dew

Tal 'omer:
Ehye katal leyisra'el yifraḥ kashoshana
Veyakh shorashav kalevanon

Yod

Yam ✽ יָם ✽ Sea

Hayamim 'omrim:
Mikolot mayim rabim 'adirim
mishberey yam
'Adir bamarom Adonai.
'Edotekha ne'emnu me'od
Levetekha na'ava kodesh
Adonai le'orekh yamim

The Seas say: With the roar of rushing waters and mighty breakers the Lord thunders on high.

הַכּוֹכָבִים אוֹמְרִים:
מוֹנֶה מִסְפָּר לַכּוֹכָבִים לְכֻלָּם שֵׁמוֹת יִקְרָא:

The Stars say:
He counts the number of the stars
and gives them all names.

Kaf

Kokhavim ✡ כּוֹכָבִים ✡ Stars

Hakokhavim 'omrim:
Mone mispar lakokhavim
Lekhulam shemot yikra.

Lamed

Laila ✡ לַיְלָה ✡ Night

Laila 'omer:
Lehagid baboker ḥasdekha
Ve'emunatkha balelot.

Night says: I proclaim Your eternal love each dawn, and Your faithfulness every night.

מִדְבָּר אֹמֵר: יְשֻׂשׂוּם מִדְבָּר וְצִיָּה וְתָגֵל עֲרָבָה וְתִפְרַח כַּחֲבַצָּלֶת:

The Desert says:
The arid desert shall be glad and the desert smile and bloom like a rose.

Mem

Midbar ✤ מִדְבָּר ✤ Desert

Midbar 'omer:
Yesusum midbar vetsiya
Vetagel 'arava vetifraḥ
kaḥavatselet.

Nun

Nesher ✦ נֶשֶׁר ✦ Eagle

Hanesher 'omer:
'Atem re'item asher 'asiti
leMitsrayim
Va'esa etkhem 'al kanfe nesharim
Va'avi etkhem 'elai.

הַנֶּשֶׁר אוֹמֵר: אַתֶּם רְאִיתֶם אֲשֶׁר עָשִׂיתִי לְמִצְרַיִם וָאֶשָּׂא אֶתְכֶם עַל־כַּנְפֵי נְשָׁרִים וָאָבִא אֶתְכֶם אֵלָי:

The eagle says: You have seen what I did to Egypt
But you I bore on eagles' wings,
and brought you to Me.

Samekh

Sus ✦ סוּס ✦ Horse

Lesusati berikhve Par'oh dimitikh ra'yati.

Ayin

Etz ✦ עֵץ ✦ Tree

Vehaya ke'etz shatul 'al mayim
ve'al yuval yeshalaḥ shorashav
velo yir'e ki yavo ḥom
vehaya 'alehu ra'anan
uvishnat batsoret lo yid'ag
velo yamish me'asot peri.

הָעֵץ אוֹמֵר

וְהָיָה כְּעֵץ שָׁתוּל עַל־מַיִם
וְעַל־יוּבַל יְשַׁלַּח שָׁרָשָׁיו
וְלֹא יִרְאֶה כִּי־יָבֹא חֹם
וְהָיָה עָלֵהוּ רַעֲנָן
וּבִשְׁנַת בַּצֹּרֶת לֹא יִדְאָג
וְלֹא יָמִישׁ מֵעֲשׂוֹת פֶּרִי:

The tree says
Israel shall be like
a tree planted by water
sending forth its
roots by a stream.
It will not feel the
coming of the heat.
Its leaves are
always fresh.
It does not worry during a year of drought,
And never stops producing fruit.

Pay

Pil פִּיל Elephant

Hapil 'omer:

Ma gadlu ma'asekha 'Adonai

Me'od 'amku maḥshevotekha.

צ

Tsadi

TSiporim ⚹ צִפּוֹרִים ⚹ Birds

Hatsiporim 'omrot:
'Ezri me'im Adonai
'Osey shamayim va'aretz.

הַצִפּוֹרִים אוֹמְרוֹת:
עֶזְרִי מֵעִם יהוה
עֹשֵׂה שָׁמַיִם וָאָרֶץ:

The birds say:
My help comes from the Lord,
Maker of Heaven and Earth.

הַקֶּשֶׁת אוֹמֶרֶת: אֶת-קַשְׁתִּי נָתַתִּי בֶּעָנָן וְהָיְתָה לְאוֹת בְּרִית בֵּינִי וּבֵין הָאָרֶץ:

The Rainbow says: "God says 'I have set my rainbow in the clouds as a sign of the covenant for all the generations to eternity.'"

Qof

Keshet ✥ קֶשֶׁת ✥ Rainbow

Hakeshet 'omeret:

Vayomer Elohim: zot 'ot habrit 'asher 'ani noten beni uvenekhem uven kol nefesh ḥaya 'asher 'itkhem ledorot 'olam.

ר

Resh

Ravnitsran shakhom

רַבְנִצְרָן שַׁחֹם

Blue Triggerfish

Haravnitsran shakhom 'omer:

Zeh hayam gadol ureḥav yadayim

Sham remes ve'en mispar

Ḥayot ketanot 'im gedolot.

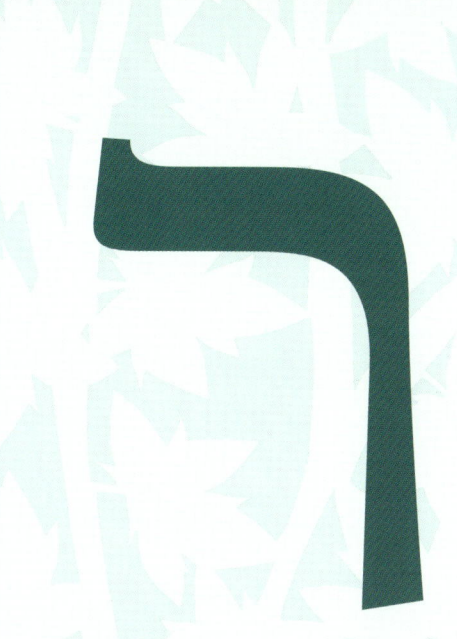

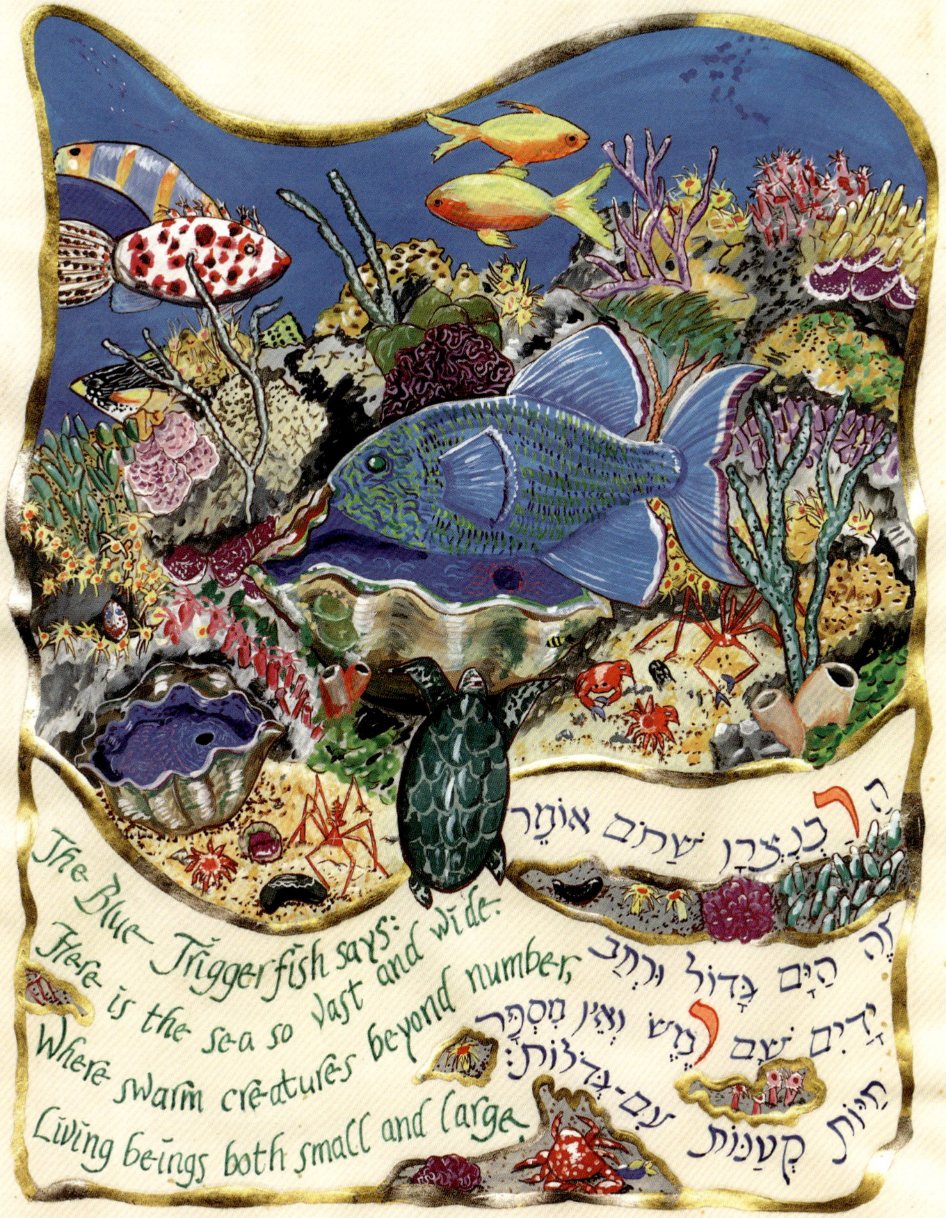
הרבנצרן שחם אומר
זה הים גדול ורחב
ידים שם רמש ואין מספר
חיות קטנות עם-גדלות:
The Blue Triggerfish says:
Here is the sea so vast and wide,
Where swarm creatures beyond number,
Living beings both small and large.

ש

Shin

Shvil heḥalav

שְׁבִיל הֶחָלָב

Milky Way

Shvil heḥalav 'omer:

Borakhi nafshi 'et 'Adonai:

'Adonai 'elohai gadalta me'od

Hod vehadar lavashta

'Ote 'or kesalma

Note shamayim kayeri'a.

Tav

Ta'im ✡ תָּאִים ✡ Cells

Kol hata'im 'omrim:
Vayar Elohim 'et kol 'asher 'asa
vehiney tov me'od.

כָּל הַתָּאִים אוֹמְרִים:
וַיַּרְא אֱלֹהִים אֶת־כָּל אֲשֶׁר עָשָׂה
וְהִנֵּה טוֹב מְאֹד
וַיְהִי־עֶרֶב
וַיְהִי־בֹקֶר יוֹם הַשִּׁשִּׁי׃

All the cells say:
God saw all that He had made
and it was indeed very good.
There was evening
and there was morning
The Sixth Day.

Kol ha'olam 'omer: Yehi kevod Adonai le'olam yismaḥ 'Adonai bema'asav.

Can you find all the letters of the *aleph-bet* hidden in these paintings?

(Hint: visit www.alltheworldpraisesyou.com for the key!)

Alef (Isaiah 24:16)

Earth says: The Earth is the Lord's
And everything it holds,
The world and all who live on it.

What do you think our Earth looks like from space? This is a picture of our planet from space, surrounded by the starry heavens. The star painting shows my version of a famous Hubble Space Telescope picture of the "extreme deep field" of outer space. This view of the stars, near and far, shows us tiny particles and rays of light arriving at our eyes and telescopes now (or in 2014 when the Hubble photograph was made), that first shone from these stars a very long time ago. In fact scientists think the light is from right after the Big Bang, the explosion that created our universe 13.7 billion years ago. Visit https://apod.nasa.gov/apod/ap140605.html to see the Hubble photograph! This verse is included in the original tenth century manuscripts of *Perek Shira*.

Bet (Psalm 135:7)

The Lightening says:
He makes the storm clouds soar
From the ends of the Earth;
He makes lightning for the rainstorm;
He releases the winds from His vaults.

Have you seen lightning bolts spark from the clouds to the ground below? Do you see how small the houses and trees are? Imagine how far the lightning must travel to reach the ground! Above the clouds we can even see the deep sky. This picture of the starry heavens comes from the same Hubble Space Telescope photograph as in the *Aleph* painting. The Hubble photograph may be found at https://apod.nasa.gov/apod/ap140605.html. This verse is included in the original tenth century manuscripts of *Perek Shira*.

Gimel (Psalm 68:10)

The rain says:
You have showered us with abundant rain, O God:
When Your land was exhausted You brought it back to life.

Can you imagine how dry and thirsty the world would be without rain? Even if rainy days sometimes stop us from playing outside, rain is important to our whole world! The clouds send us cool rain that refreshes the dry grass, waters the trees, and fills the streams and ponds so that animals can drink and wash. The rains come to the hot, dry veldt, or grasslands, of southern Africa and fill the watering holes and water the ground. Then, all its animals—elephants, zebras, birds and others, crowd around to drink, wash away the dust and play while the grasses and trees spring again to life. How could the animals drink and find grass to eat without rain? Just like the thirsty animals and plants, we are also grateful to God for the rain! This verse is included in the original tenth century manuscripts of *Perek Shira*.

Daled (Psalm 104:31)

The grass says:
May the glory of the Lord last forever;
May the Lord rejoice in His own deeds.

Do you like to look deep into the blades of grass to see all the tiny things living there? When I was a child burrowing through the grass to find the tiny flowers, insects, worms, and sometimes, if I was really lucky, even tiny lizards, was just about the most fascinating thing in the world to me. I have always marveled at the variety of life one can find in these most ordinary places. The composer of Psalm 104 seems to have had the same sense of amazement at God's greatness and interest in creating such a wide variety of life. This verse is included in the original tenth century manuscripts of *Perek Shira*.

He (Psalm 145:5)
Splendor declares:
I shall recite the majestic glory of your splendor, and your wonderful deeds.

What do you think is the biggest, most powerful, most brilliant sight in the world? To me, it's the strange and splendid Aurora Borealis, or Northern Lights, a shower of colored light that shines in the night sky over the northern part of the Earth. Auroras happen when certain kinds of electricity from the sun bounce against the outer part of Earth's atmosphere—the blanket of air covering our planet—near the North Pole. When this same beautiful light show happens near the South Pole, it is called the Aurora Australis, or Southern Lights. Whether the lights come from the north or the south, the aurora shines like a splendid crown in the night sky, and reminds us of God's own brilliant splendor. You may find a photo of the Aurora at https://apod.nasa.gov/apod/ap040730.html.

Vav (Genesis 1:11)

The rose says: God said, "Let the earth sprout vegetation, seed-bearing plants,
And fruit trees of every kind on the earth."

Can you see the honeybee zooming toward the rose bush that climbs up the tree? The tree is covered with sweet apricots that some child might enjoy soon, and sweet-smelling lilies, and bright dahlias grow from its roots. The hills in the distance are full of vineyards bursting with grape vines. Does that white dove carrying an olive twig remind you of Noah's dove? Just as after the Flood, nature restarts itself time after time through the power of seeds. Like the grass below, all of these plants have seeds that will grow into more roses and apricots, grapes and olives, just as sweet and fragrant as the ones painted here. How lucky we are that the world God created gives us these beautiful plants!

Zayin (Psalm 128:3)

The Olive Tree says:
May your wife be like a fruitful vine over your home;
your children, like olive shoots around your table.

Imagine that you are a big tree—wouldn't you like to have lots of your sprouts surrounding you? Olive trees send up many little shoots from their roots, which must have reminded the person who wrote the psalm of children gathered around their family dinner table—just like a mother surrounded by her children made him think of ripe, sweet clusters of grapes. And mothers and fathers thank God for all their children! The painting shows us a window into a family dining room with children gathered around the table, and beside the window, an olive tree surrounded by its growing shoots.

What's This?

I created *All the World Praises You* to celebrate the birth of my first grandchild, Dalia, and have smiled through every minute of the work! Dalia's great-grandfather, the celebrated scholar of Hebrew literature, Arnold J. Band, prepared the Hebrew translations and transliterations. You will see below how Dalia and I join you on every page!

All the World Praises You is inspired by the tenth century work, *Perek Shira* (Chapter of Song), an anthology of eighty-five verses praising God taken from passages throughout the Hebrew Bible, with a few passages of later sacred texts. As in *Perek Shira*, the verses in this book are placed into the mouths of a variety of natural phenomena. However, I have shortened the original anthology to create an "*aleph-bet*" book to introduce children of all ages not only to the Hebrew alphabet (the *aleph-bet*), to basic concepts of Jewish prayer and praise of God, and to our own society's important environmental awareness that we humans live together with all of Nature on the big "blue marble" of Earth. In addition, the twenty-five paintings and one paper-cut presented here introduce your child to one of the great Jewish art traditions, that of the Hebrew (and here, English) illuminated book. Since the development of the bound book, around the fourth century, the tradition of text illumination—illustrating and decorating the beloved words with gold and color—has honored Jewish sacred books such as *haggadot* and prayer books by turning every thought and word into a precious and intimate work of visual art; Christianity and Islam enjoy similar grand traditions. These illuminated paintings are created on kosher calfskin vellum, with ink, gouache (opaque watercolor), and gold and palladium leaf.

The paintings that I offer you here can be read and enjoyed by people at many different ages and different familiarity with Jewish text and lore. The notes below provide information and discussion questions about the paintings and biblical verses geared for parents reading to young children. Materials appropriate for elementary school-age students, for Bar/Bat Mitzvah age students, and for adults, in particular for *havurot* (prayer groups) discussions are available at www.AllTheWorldPraisesYou.com. There you will find commentaries that explain the paintings' visual symbolism, related biblical allusions and texts, and points for discussion. These web materials include thumbnails of the paintings, but you will need to have the book with you to see the pictures properly. Transliterations of the Hebrew are offered adjacent to each painting.

Can you find the dahlias and honeybees? You will find a dahlia and a honeybee somewhere in each painting—often well hidden! These play on the custom of medieval Jewish scribes, the people who copied Jewish books before the invention of printing, who often included their names in a simple statement or word-puzzle called a colophon at the end of their handwritten books. Since my name, Debra, is an anglicization of the Hebrew word for honeybee, *devorah*, and since this book celebrates Dalia's birth, I have turned this colophon custom into a hidden-picture game throughout the book. Somewhere in each painting you'll find a honeybee and a dahlia, sometimes very small! In the final two paintings you can find not only the hidden pictures of the dahlia and honeybee, but also of each of the Hebrew letters.

Have fun!

praising God's beauty and God's power to overturn the Egyptian army with God's mere presence when it threatened us.

Ayin (Jeremiah 17:8)

The tree says: Israel shall be like a tree planted by the water,
Sending forth its roots by a stream.
He will not feel the coming of the heat.
His leaves are always fresh.
He does not worry during a year of drought,
And never stops producing fruit.

Do you love to reach up and touch a tree's fresh, sweet-smelling leaves? This tree grows beside a stream in a city park, its lush green branches waving gently in a breeze. It reminds us of how God's nearness to us protects us as we grow up. Just like God's world sends the tree the rain that it needs, our world gives us what we need to live healthy and fruitful lives.

Pay (Psalm 92:6)

The elephant says: How great are your works, God,
Your thoughts are very deep!

When you visit the zoo, do you enjoy hearing the elephants trumpeting? The African elephant, one of the biggest and most intelligent of all creatures on earth, trumpets that God is even larger and deeper-thinking than she is! I imagine my little cockatiel, Peaches, sitting on top of the huge elephant's ear, just like he perches on my shoulder and sings his silly songs into my ear. This verse is included in the original tenth century manuscripts of *Perek Shira*.

Tsadi (Psalm 121:2)

The birds say: My help comes from the Lord,
Maker of heaven and earth.

Do you ever dream of what it must be like to be a bird? Birds in all their beauty and wild variety fly freely across sea, land and sky, nest in trees and grasses, fish, hunt and even sip from flowers. Their noisy shrieks, songs and twittering seem to sing of the joy of their free, but fragile lives in the world that God made for all of us to share.

Qof (Genesis 9:13)

The Rainbow says: "God says "I have set my rainbow in the clouds
As a sign of the covenant
For all generations to eternity."

I love to see a rainbow after a rainstorm! Do you? After seeing Noah and all his family and animals in his ark to safety after the Flood, God lit the sky with a rainbow as a promise to all generations of people and life on Earth, that God would never again allow such destruction.

Resh (Psalm 104:25)

The Blue Triggerfish says:
Here is the sea so vast and wide.
Where swarm creatures beyond number,
Living beings both small and large.

Have you ever had a chance to wade around tidepools, or seen films about the coral reefs? We thank God for the many kinds of creatures swarming and swimming around our Earth's precious coral reefs, with their wild variety of shapes, colors and habits. The large Blue Triggerfish in the center of this painting lives in the Red Sea coral reef off the coast of Eilat, Israel. The sea creatures in this painting live there and in other important coral reefs, such Australia's Great Barrier Reef, and the Belize Barrier Reef. Can you find a coral that looks like a dahlia, and a fish that looks like a honeybee?

Shin (Psalm 104:1)

The Milky Way says:
O my soul, bless the Lord:
"Lord, my God, You are very great.
You are clothed in glory and majesty;
Wrapped in light like a robe,
You spread the heavens like a tent."

Have you ever looked up at the sky late on a clear night, in a place far from the lights of our cities? If so, you may have felt wrapped up in a blanket of stars, like the composer of this psalm did when he thanked God for giving us the glittering night sky. When it's dark enough you can see the blanket of light that we call The Milky Way stretching across the whole sky. You can only imagine how enormous God must be to create a blanket so big! The starlight looks silvery, but the light the stars send to us is really made up of a whole rainbow of colors.

Tav (Genesis 1:31)

All the cells say:
God saw all that He had made,
And it was indeed very good.
There was evening and there was morning:
The Sixth Day.

What do you think that a flower, or your skin is made from? All of us living on Earth need every other kind of life on our planet. We all thank God for the huge variety of life that our Earth has developed. And every part of all our bodies—whether we are plants, animals, fungus or bacteria—are made of many kinds of tiny cells that work together to help us live. Here the petals of the small dahlia come together from millions of much tinier cells, and in the bottom right corner we see what the honeybee's eye looks like under a microscope. The picture shows some of the millions of cells that take in the light and shapes of the world she sees.

FINAL VERSE (Psalm 104:31)

All the world says:
May the glory of the Lord endure forever!
May the Lord rejoice in His works!

Every day and every night all of us who live together on Earth, every kind of plant and animal, each in our own way, is happy to be living in the beautiful world that God brought into being! In these paintings of a daytime and nighttime forest, I have hidden all the Hebrew letters that make up our names. Can you find the letters? (Hint: you'll find the key to these puzzles at www.AllTheWorldPraisesYou.com). Every one of us, whatever our name may be, has an important part in the life of our amazing planet Earth!

Ḥet (Psalm 104:24)

The Beetle says:
How many are your deeds, O Lord!
You did them all with wisdom.
The earth swarms with your creatures.

Have you ever found a ladybug on your arm, watched a butterfly emerging from a cocoon, or been amazed at all the colors and shapes of beetles or worms? Just think of how different fireflies and cockroaches are—and they're both beetles! I think that the composer of Psalm 104 was amazed at God's ability to make so many different insects and other small creatures to crawl or fly around the land, even ones so small or so common that we often barely notice them.

Tet (Hosea 14:6)
The Dew says:
I shall be like gentle dew to Israel.
It shall blossom like a lily,
And strike root like a cedar.

Have you ever touched the delicate dewdrops on the grass in the morning? God promised to treat Israel as softly and gently as the dew forms on the plants at night, like the tenderness of a parent toward a child. That tenderness makes us as strong as the roots of a tall cedar tree. A beautiful lily plant, covered in morning dewdrops, opens its flowers between the roots of a strong tree. That same tenderness brings out the beauty that is within every child. The lily's sweet scent attracts a honeybee—while a little dahlia bud prepares to bloom at its side. This verse is included in the original tenth century manuscripts of *Perek Shira*.

Yod (Psalm 93:3)

The Seas say:
With the roar of rushing waters and mighty breakers
The Lord thunders on high.

Have you been near the beach during a storm? Usually the calm water reflects the sky's peaceful blue and gray, but when the wind blows hard the waves also toss and roar wildly. The Hebrew word for wind is *ruaḥ*. Since *ruaḥ* is also the Hebrew word for God's spirit, the composer of this psalm may have imagined God's voice roaring like the ocean waves. Can you see the dahlia bouncing in the waves like a beachball? This verse is included in the original tenth century manuscripts of *Perek Shira*.

Kaf (Psalm 147:4)
The stars say:
He counts the number of the stars
And gives them all names.

Can you count all the stars in the sky? One of the ways that God tells us that God is bigger and more powerful than any other being is by gently challenging Abraham to count the number of the stars—he can't! The poet tells us that only God has clear enough vision to count and organize all the lights that sparkle in our night sky, and only God cares enough, like a shepherd for his sheep, to give each of them a name. The constellations of stars in this painting were visible in the sky over Washington, D.C. at the moment that Dalia was born. The rainbow-colored border represents the light spectrum, all the colors of light—red, orange, yellow, green, blue, indigo and violet—produced by the chemistry inside the stars that we see in the sky.

Lamed (Psalm 92:3)

Night says:
I proclaim your eternal love each dawn
And your faithfulness every night.

When you go to bed at night, do you feel your parents' love all around you? The night sky stretches from sunset at right to sunrise at left, and we can imagine God wrapped all around us. The sky shows the moon and stars as they in its phase the night Dalia was born, and, as in the last painting, the constellations visible in the sky. Besides the moon and constellations, the painting shows a picture of deep outer space based on the same Hubble Space Telescope photograph described in the *Alef* painting, reminding us that as we peer through the night we can almost see the beginnings of the amazing universe that God created for us. This verse is included in the original tenth century manuscripts of *Perek Shira*.

Mem (Isaiah 35:1)

The desert says: The arid desert shall be glad, the desert smile and bloom like a rose.

Have you ever taken a walk in a desert? When Dalia's dad was growing up in San Diego, our family took a day-hike in the California desert every spring. The winter rains had just ended, the soil and plants were refreshed, and the cactus bloomed wildly. All the vibrant reds, oranges and yellows of the flowers shone bright against the pale soil and deep blue sky. After the winter rain, the desert really seemed to smile! Living in hot and dry Israel, the composer of these words knew that rain is a precious blessing, God's special gift for us! This verse is included in the original tenth century manuscripts of *Perek Shira*.

Nun (Exodus 19:4)

The eagle says: You have seen what I did to Egypt
But you I bore on eagles' wings
And brought you to Me.

Have you seen an eagle soaring through the sky? When Moses saw the strong golden eagle that lives in the Middle East spreading its wide wings over the Red Sea and the desert, he was reminded of God's protection of Israel as it escaped slavery. Can you imagine how tiny the gigantic pyramid looks from the eagle's height? Can you see the tiny people on the ground? How easily they could imagine that God flew overhead just like the powerful eagle!

Samekh (The Song of Songs 1:9)

The Horse says: "Solomon writes:
'My beloved,
I compare you to a mare
Among the stallions of Pharoah's chariots.'"

Have you ever seen a beautiful horse running through a field? When this strong Egyptian chariot stallion sees a beautiful mare running free past his stable, he jumps up with such excitement that he might overturn his chariot! In ancient Israel, where horses were very rare, we only knew these beautiful and powerful animals as part of strong foreign armies, such as Egypt's. Instead of horses, we had donkeys for riding and pulling our carts. The early rabbis thought of the beautiful love poetry in The Song of Songs as a love-song to God. Here they thought that young King Solomon was actually

Debra Band draws upon her love of both the manuscript arts and Jewish texts and tradition in her Hebrew/English illuminated manuscripts. She is the author and illuminator of *The Song of Songs: The Honeybee in the Garden* (Jewish Publication Society, 2005), *I Will Wake the Dawn: Illuminated Psalms* (Jewish Publication Society, 2007), *Arise! Arise! Deborah, Ruth and Hannah* (Honeybee in the Garden, 2012) the latter two, in collaboration with Arnold J. Band, and *Kabbalat Shabbat: the Grand Unification* (Honeybee in the Garden, 2016). Debra's work is collected and exhibited across the world. She has lived throughout the United States and Canada, and resides in the Washington, D.C. area with her husband, Michael Diamond, and menagerie...not far from her first grandchild, Dalia. More information about her work may be found at www.dbandart.com.

Arnold J. Band was Professor of Hebrew and Comparative Literature at UCLA from 1959 to 2016. He has authored many books on S.Y. Agnon and Naḥman of Bratslav, and many scholarly articles in both Hebrew and English, some collected in two volumes. He has received many honors for his contributions to Jewish studies across the world. Band is the founder of the Department of Comparative Literature and the Center for Jewish Studies at UCLA.

All the World Praises You, which celebrates their first grandchild and great-grandchild respectively, is their third collaboration.